Side Effects

A comedy

Eric Chappell

Samuel French — London
www.samuelfrench-london.co.uk

SIDE EFFECTS

First presented on 28th September 2011 by The Robin Hood Theatre Company On Tour at Farndon Memorial Hall with the following cast:

Frank Cook	Jonty Redgrave
June Cook	Sally Williams
Rev. Paul Latimer	Nick Timms
Sarah Latimer	Rebecca Smith
Tracey	Lindsay Follen

Directed by Dawn Bond
Designed by Paul Stubbs
Lighting design by Dave Baliol-Key

COPYRIGHT INFORMATION

(See also page ii)

CHARACTERS

Frank Cook, 50s. A recent invalid and resentful of
his condition. Anti-clerical

June Cook, his wife. A few years younger than
Frank. She is long-suffering, frustrated,
but with a wry sense of humour.

Rev. Paul Latimer, 40s. The recipient of a heart
transplant. Superficially confident but at
breaking point. Inclined to be priggish and
judgmental

Sarah Latimer, his wife, 40s. Relentlessly middle-
class. A cut glass voice and rather precious
but not a fool.

Tracey, 20s. Attractive, solemn and mysterious. A
catalyst.

SYNOPSIS OF SCENES

The action of the play takes place in the visitors' room
of a convalescent home.

ACT I
SCENE 1 Early evening in late summer
SCENE 2 An hour later

ACT II
SCENE 1 The following evening
SCENE 2 An afternoon in summer

Time — the present

Other plays by Eric Chappell
published by Samuel French Ltd:

Cut and Dried
Double Vision
False Pretences
Father's Day
Fiddlers Three (comprising Cut and Dried
and We Don't Want To Lose You)
Haunted
Haywire
Heatstroke
It Can Damage Your Health
Natural Causes
Rising Damp
Something's Burning
Summer End
Theft
Up and Coming
We Don't Want To Lose You
Wife After Death

ACT I

The visitors' room of a convalescent home. An early evening in late summer

The room contains easy chairs, a stool and a couple of coffee tables. There is a desk and a bookcase. A pair of crutches and a collapsed wheelchair lean against the wall. There is a thermos jug of water and some glasses on the tables, a bowl of flowers and a handbell. Upstage is a glass door leading out into the gardens. There are heavy curtains either side of the door. A second door, L, leads to the hall

Frank Cook, a man in his fifties, enters from the hall. He is leaning on a walking frame. He regards the room with a sour expression. He crosses and looks out into the gardens. He sits. He regards a heavy volume left on the coffee table. He tries to lift it with one hand. Fails. He tries to lift it with both hands but the book still falls from his grasp. He sits back with a sigh. He uses both hands to lift his leg on to the stool

Paul Latimer enters from the garden. He is a few years younger than Frank. He is tall, pale and distinguished. Despite the warm evening he is wearing an overcoat and scarf

Frank This the visitors' room?
Paul I believe so.
Frank They can't be expecting many visitors.
Paul There is the lounge ...
Frank Have you seen them in there? I was hoping for a little female companionship — a mild flirtation. Not much chance of that. We'll all be singing hymns. We shouldn't be in a place like this — we're too young.
Paul I'm only here for a few days.
Frank Same here. Respite?
Paul Sorry?
Frank Giving your wife a rest?
Paul Yes. We're just moving in. I've been in hospital and ——
Frank We're having a stairlift fitted. I used to take those steps two at a time. Now I'm sleeping in the study. She says she wants me back —

the truth is she wants the study back. If she's hoping for anything else she's going to be disappointed.

Paul looks embarrassed and becomes engrossed in the bookcase

Do you get that feeling sometimes?

Paul What feeling?

Frank That you've become a burden?

Paul Sometimes. But they also serve ...

Frank Serve?

Paul "They also serve who only stand and wait."

Frank But I'm not standing, am I? Standing would be a treat. I said to June, that's my wife, put me out with the rubbish. Do you know what she said? Would that be the grey bin or the black bin. She has quite a sense of humour.

Paul (*drily*) She probably needs it.

Frank What?

Paul One does in these situations.

Frank Yes, she has a sense of humour — if a little barbed. Of course, it's meant to spur me on.

Paul I suppose she's trying to lift your spirits. After all, there are people worse off.

Frank Are there? I don't come across them.

Paul I think you'll find them in the lounge.

Frank But they've got one foot in the grave already. I was playing five sets of tennis last year.

Paul Is it some sort of paralysis?

Frank (*concerned*) Paralysis! They didn't say anything about paralysis. Do I look paralysed?

Paul I'm not sure. Did they say what it was?

Frank They did but I can't tell you.

Paul Why not?

Frank I can't pronounce it. Neither can they. They use letters. They said it's not life threatening. I said, "call this a life?"

Paul Did they say anything else?

Frank They don't know anything else. I go privately for all this advice and all I get is a friendly pat on the shoulder as I go out the door. They did tell me one thing — it affects one in a hundred thousand.

Paul And I suppose you're thinking, why me?

Frank No, I'm thinking why not one of the others. One of those in the lounge for example — they wouldn't even notice it.

Paul I suppose you were chosen.

Frank Chosen?

Paul There's often a purpose although we don't always see it.

Frank What purpose? Lift that book.
Paul (*puzzled*) What?

Frank points to the thick volume on the table

Frank The one on the coffee table.

Paul picks up the book

You can lift it with one hand. I can't lift it with two! Last year I carried a fridge to the end of the drive. Now I can't even pull a cork. What purpose is there in that?
Paul As I said the purpose isn't always clear. You may come through this a better person.
Frank I didn't need this to make me a better person. I was doing all right. (*Eyeing Paul narrowly*) Were you smoking out there?
Paul (*uneasily*) Yes. A recent weakness I'm afraid. I don't know why, I suppose it's to calm my nerves. It was a sudden craving.
Frank They also serve who only stand and smoke.
Paul (*smiling*) You could say that.
Frank At least you can walk.
Paul Yes.
Frank Was it heart?
Paul If you don't mind — I try to avoid talking about it. I don't want people thinking I'm an invalid.
Frank I'm the same. People keep asking me but I don't like to talk about it.
Paul Is there a cure?
Frank If there is they haven't mentioned it. No, we're reduced to prayer at the moment. My wife's praying for me, her sewing circle's praying for me, her mother's praying for me — at least she says she is. Even Aunt Marion in South Africa's praying for me. What good that'll do I don't know — she can't even get through on the phone. They're all at it. And it's all a waste of time.
Paul You don't believe in the power of prayer?
Frank My wife does. She's a regular churchgoer. She's always been gullible.
Paul But you're not.
Frank Mumbo-jumbo. And if she's so confident why is she having the stairlift fitted? She's obviously expecting a long haul despite the prayers, I think she looks upon this as judgement.
Paul A judgement?
Frank A punishment.
Paul For not going to church?

Frank (*broodingly*) For everything. She's been waiting for a big finger to come out of the sky and squash me for years. Well, I may not be perfect but I never neglected the family. Two girls — never wanted for a thing — both had ponies. Never see them now. They say I've become bitter and twisted. I may have become twisted but I've never allowed myself to become bitter.

Paul hides a smile

Do you think it's a punishment?
Paul Perhaps. But not from God. Perhaps you're punishing yourself.
Frank (*frowning*) What do you mean? Are you suggesting it's all in the mind?
Paul The mind can affect the body.
Frank (*sharply*) You think I'm making this up?
Paul No.
Frank Are you a psychiatrist?
Paul Good heavens, no.
Frank I thought not.

Sound of church bells. Frank listens

Doesn't that get on your nerves?
Paul I quite like it. A warm Sunday evening and the sound of church bells across the meadow. "The holy time as quiet as a nun."

Frank stares at him curiously

Frank It's certainly music to my wife's ears. She'd be there now with the rest of the phonies if she wasn't coming to see me. Although they're without a vicar at the moment. The last one left in a hurry.
Paul Why was that?
Frank Came into money — they found his cassock half way down the drive.
Paul (*smiling*) Do you believe that?
Frank Perhaps you'll believe this when it comes out. (*Confidentially*) He had this old lady's Chippendale furniture. Said she left it to him on her death bed. The family are contesting it. Every sick visit he left with a chair. (*Pause*) Aren't you warm in that coat?
Paul They tell me I have to be careful. I must avoid chills. Apparently my immunity system has been comprised.
Frank Tell me about it. I've had cellulitis, water infection, and shingles all in the last six months. But it doesn't pay to pamper yourself.

Paul Perhaps you're right ... (*He removes his coat and scarf and hangs them on a peg. He turns to reveal that he's wearing a clerical collar*)

Frank's mouth drops open. For once he's speechless

(*Smiling*) Now, if you'll excuse me, I've promised to conduct the service tonight — for the rest of the phonies ...

Paul exits into the hall

Frank still can't believe what has happened. He struggles towards the door

At the same time June, his wife, enters. She is considerably younger than her husband. She has a bright attractive smile. She is carrying a shopping bag

June Moving around — that's good. Have you settled in?
Frank Yes — right up to my neck.
June What do you mean?
Frank I've just insulted a fellow guest.
June Already! You've only been here five minutes! Insulted him, are you sure?
Frank Well, let's put it this way — he won't be passing me the cruet at dinner. I didn't know he was a man of the cloth.
June You mean the Reverend Latimer?
Frank You know him?
June Yes. I saw him in the hall. He's our new vicar. He's here for a few days respite. He's had major surgery. Frank, what did you say to him?
Frank It was nothing personal. I was just being myself.
June Being yourself. That's fatal.
Frank We were having a friendly chat and he suddenly whipped off his scarf and revealed himself. If I'd have known I wouldn't have said ...
June What?
Frank What I said ...
June So he wasn't the only one who revealed himself.
Frank (*accusingly*) Did you know he was here?
June (*uneasily*) I wasn't absolutely sure ...
Frank Yes, you were. What's this all about? Do you think he'll be a good influence?
June I wasn't expecting miracles, Frank.
Frank Weren't you? I thought you believed in them. Have you talked to him about me?
June No.

Frank Are you sure?

June Frank, I don't talk to anyone about you.

Frank Are you ashamed of me?

June Yes. When you insult people.

Frank I didn't insult him.

June You said you did.

Frank Only indirectly. So that's it! I've got you, your mother, the stitch-and-bitch club, Aunt Marion in South Africa, and now him. A vicar who also thinks he's a psychiatrist. Apparently it's not God who's punishing me — I'm punishing myself. In which case I must be a bloody masochist! He's also very underhand.

June He's not.

Frank He was. Underhand and dodgy.

June Dodgy! You've only known him five minutes.

Frank And how well do you know him?

June Well, I know Sarah better. She's his wife. I've been helping her to move in.

Frank You're quite a friend of the family then.

June I wouldn't say that. I've heard him preach. He's wonderful, so charismatic. He's not dodgy.

Frank Did you know that he smokes?

June (*surprised*) No.

Frank Out there behind the bushes, having a crafty drag. Where's his will power? I gave up thirty years ago. Where's his self-control?

June I know why you're annoyed with him. Because he dared to suggest that your illness may be psychosomatic.

Frank Psycho-what?

June Self inflicted. That you're tortured with guilt.

Frank I am not tortured with —— . Have you been talking to him?

June No.

Frank (*after a pause*) So he's had major surgery. What's so special about that?

June You haven't had it.

Frank Excuse me, I'll have a leg off.

June Frank, he's got more to worry about than your immortal soul.

Frank Oh, I don't know. Isn't the lost lamb worth all the flock?

June I don't think anyone could call you a lamb, lost or otherwise.

Frank What do you mean he's got more to worry about?

June Sarah's very concerned about him. We all are.

Frank If you're going to be concerned, be concerned about me! I'm turning into a tadpole. First the legs — now the arms.

June (*concerned*) The arms?

Frank (*seriously*) I couldn't raise myself up this morning. I couldn't even lift that book.

June (*distressed*) Oh, Cookie. (*She puts her arms about his shoulders*)
And you're losing weight. I can feel your shoulder blades.

Frank A tadpole doesn't have shoulder blades. All I'll have is a wiggle.
Those tablets aren't working.

June Give them time.

Frank A tadpole hasn't got time.

June You're not a tadpole. So don't go on about it.

Frank (*studying her*) You're fed up with me aren't you?

June No.

Frank I'm a dead weight.

June You're not a dead weight.

Frank I'm a liability.

June You're not a liability, Cookie.

Frank I am. You're tired of me. You didn't sign on for this.

June I'm not tired of you.

Frank Next time you take me for a drive — leave me by the roadside.

June I would but there's a law against fly-tipping.

Frank Is that meant to be funny?

June I'm trying to cheer you up ... I don't want you feeling sorry for
yourself.

Frank Your words of sympathy bring tears to my eyes.

June It doesn't take much.

Frank What do you mean?

June A few words of sympathy and you're blubbering.

Frank I am not!

June When anyone rings to ask how you are — you have to put the
phone down and inhale.

Frank I don't.

June They can hear you choking.

Frank If I'm moved by their words of sympathy, is that surprising? I
hear them so seldom.

June I'm sympathetic.

Frank Are you? When you answer the phone what do you say? "Oh,
he's fine."

June That's because I want you to be fine. You used to be fine.

Frank Well, I'm not now. I have all the life and vitality of a vegetable
marrow.

June Then you can come to church next week. It's Harvest Festival.

Frank I wondered how long it would be before you mentioned church.

June It was a joke. I just don't want you feeling sorry for yourself.

Frank If I feel sorry for myself I'm the only one who does. Where are
the girls?

June They couldn't make it.

Frank Frightened that they'd have to push the wheelchair. They couldn't — they're too fat.

June They're not fat.

Frank We've fed them too well. They'd split a gusset.

June They don't come because you're so angry and bitter all the time. They don't know what to say to you.

Frank Oh, they know what to say — they're just frightened of saying it. They're afraid I'll cut them out of the will.

June You're doing it again. You're writing yourself off. Where's your fighting spirit? You have to fight, Frank.

Frank Why? What's spirit got to do with it? People with spirit are dropping like flies. I carried a fridge to the end of the drive last year — now look at me.

June It's important that you have the right attitude. Everyone says ——

Frank Everyone? Where did these words of wisdom come from? The stitch-and-bitch club? Did they come out with this whilst running off a few kneelers?

June They think if you found your faith ——

Frank Find it! I haven't lost it. I never had it.

June Don't say that. You know how it distresses me.

Frank I don't care. (*After a pause*) And I'm not going to Walsingham.

June It's only a bus trip.

Frank It's faith healing. Are we all going to throw our crutches in the air and dance in a circle?

June I'm not expecting a cure. I thought it would be nice to do something together. We do nothing together.

Frank We can't.

June puts her arms around him

June We'll have the stairlift in next week ...

Frank Oh, yes?

June We'll be together again.

Frank I wouldn't raise your hopes. You won't get much life out of a vegetable marrow.

June You're not a vegetable marrow.

Frank Have you seen it lately? I've seen bigger acorns.

June (*sighing*) Now you're an acorn. Never mind, Cookie, great oaks from little acorns grow. (*She kisses him on the cheek*)

Frank If you're expecting a great oak you will be disappointed.

June Frank, it's time we returned to a normal life.

Frank I'm not normal!

June Yes, you are. It's time you got back to the office. There's nothing wrong with your brain.

Frank How do I get there? Or do I send my brain up in a jar?

June You could travel in the guard's van.

Frank I'm not travelling in the guard's van! Everyone will see me. And what about the tube? Have you seen those commuters? They're like rats leaving a sinking ship. They'll upturn the chair and kick my spokes in. Commuters don't have any pity.

June All right. If you don't want to go back to the office — let's take that holiday.

Frank What holiday?

June We were going to Egypt.

Frank Egypt?

June The pyramids.

Frank The pyramids — in a wheelchair?

June Why not?

Frank I'll tell you why not. I'll be up to my axles in sand and some fundamentalist will come along and stick a bomb up my arse.

June He wouldn't. He'd think you'd been afflicted by God.

Frank So you do think it's a judgement.

June No.

Frank That's why you chose this place. So I could meet the vicar. Well, I don't want to meet him.

June Why not?

Frank Because he's a canting hypocrite.

June You've only just met him. You've never heard him cant! Why don't you come to the service tonight? It'll be quite short, quite informal.

Frank No.

June It's not church.

Frank No. There'll be praying.

June You need all the prayers you can get.

Frank Not tonight. Where did he come from?

June Who?

Frank The Reverend Latimer.

June The cathedral. He was a member of the Chapter. He was very highly regarded. He was destined for high office until ...

Frank Until what?

June He became ill. They sent him here for a rest.

Frank Why did they send him here? There are plenty of soft jobs within the cathedral.

June They thought the country air would do him good.

Frank Well, I think it's ——

June Dodgy?

Frank Strange.

June Well, if you're not coming ... (*She moves towards the door*) If you see Sarah, tell her I've gone through.

Frank Sarah? What's she like?

June (*smiling*) She says she's not your typical vicar's wife but she is. Daughter of a bishop, raised behind high walls, played with the gardener's boy, had a pony called Muffin. But I like her. (*She pauses by the door*) Why don't you try a walk around the garden?

Frank I couldn't get the walker through the door.

June Try those crutches.

Frank They're not mine.

June They won't mind.

Frank I couldn't manage the step.

June You could. Remember the bad leg first.

Frank They're both bad.

June The bad one downwards ... the good one upwards. Remember what the physio said. The bad one to hell, the good one to heaven.

Frank I knew you'd bring religion into it.

June sighs and exits into the hall

Frank struggles to his feet. He studies the door and then the crutches. Finally he decides. He takes up the crutches and leans on them. He makes for the door. To his horror one of the crutches begins to telescope. He leans further and further to one side almost keeling over

Tracey enters from the garden. She is in her late 20s, attractive, rather solemn. Her dress is low cut and she has an abundance of jewellery. When she speaks her voice is low and serious

They regard each other. She notes Frank's acute angle

Tracey Are you all right?

Frank Fine.

Tracey (*sympathetically*) Have you got one leg shorter than the other?

Frank No.

Tracey I had a friend who had one leg shorter than the other.

Frank I haven't got one leg shorter than the other.

Tracey He had a special shoe ——

Frank throws the crutches aside and sits

Frank Are you looking for someone?

Tracey Yes. The vicar.

Frank becomes interested

Frank He was here a minute ago.
Tracey I thought so. I can sense his presence.
Frank That's the cigarette smoke. It clings. (*Pause*) You're younger than I thought.
Tracey Has he mentioned me?
Frank No. My wife has.
Tracey (*surprised*) Has she?
Frank I suppose you'd like him to give it up?
Tracey What?
Frank Smoking.
Tracey No.
Frank Oh.
Tracey I'm probably the cause of it.
Frank Do you smoke?
Tracey No.

Frank watches her as she jangles around the room picking up objects and examining them thoughtfully

Frank I must say you're not the typical vicar's wife.
Tracey I'm not his wife.
Frank What?
Tracey As for not being typical — that's for others to say.

Frank's interest grows

Frank You're not Sarah?
Tracey No, I'm Tracey. (*Cautiously*) Is she here?
Frank Who?
Tracey His wife.
Frank No, but she's expected
Tracey Oh. (*She begins to move towards the garden*)

Frank studies her

Frank You said you were the cause of it.
Tracey What?
Frank His smoking.
Tracey I make him nervous.
Frank Why is that?
Tracey He never smoked until he met me.
Frank Where did you meet?
Tracey I met him when he was at the cathedral.
Frank So you've come quite a way.

Tracey Yes.

He watches her as she moves around the room, mysteriously picking up objects and putting them down

Frank Did you know him well?
Tracey (*turning*) Why did you ask that?
Frank You followed him here.
Tracey (*after a pause*) He has something that belongs to me.
Frank (*smiling*) Where have I heard that before? Was it left to him?
Tracey Yes. It belonged to a very dear friend of mine.
Frank And now he's got it.
Tracey Yes.
Frank You won't get it back. They hang on to things. It's known as the clergyman's grip.
Tracey I just want to share it.
Frank But he doesn't want to?
Tracey No.
Frank Is it valuable?
Tracey It is to me.
Frank Then you've seen the last of it. And he'll be preaching a sermon on avarice next Sunday.
Tracey He was lovely to me at first.
Frank Was he?
Tracey So understanding.
Frank I'm sure he was. (*He steals a glance at her cleavage*) How was he understanding?
Tracey He was kind. We'd go for long walks.
Frank That must have raised a few eyebrows.
Tracey It did. (*She lowers her voice*) Look, if you have a chance to speak to the vicar ...
Frank Yes?
Tracey Alone ...
Frank Alone? Of course.
Tracey Tell him, I'll be out there on the bench. (*She glances towards the hall and listens*) I think she's here. I'd better go. (*She pauses by the garden door. She inhales deeply and smiles*) I know what it is. It's not tobacco — it's diesel oil.

Tracey exits

Frank stares after her

Frank Diesel oil?

He listens. He hears voices from the hall. He rubs his hands gleefully

June enters leading Sarah Latimer

Sarah has a nice figure but her general appearance is a little smudged. Her hair is slightly unkempt. Her good skirt and jacket rather creased. She has the air of someone who does things in a hurry

June Sarah, this is my husband ...
Sarah Ah, Mr Cook, I've heard so much about you ...

Frank shoots a glance at June

Frank Nothing good I hope.
June (*uneasily*) Frank ...
Sarah Please, don't get up, Frank.
Frank I wasn't going to. I can't.
Sarah I do understand.
Frank Do you? I wish I did.
June (*with emphasis*) Frank, this is Sarah — the vicar's wife.
Frank Oh, that's a surprise ... (*He looks towards the garden as if confused*)

June eyes him suspiciously

Sarah (*smiling*) I know what you're thinking.
Frank You do?
Sarah Not your typical vicar's wife. No brave little hats and knitted gloves. I've quite scandalised the congregation with my necklines. But as I said to the Bishop why should the devil have the pick of the wardrobe?
June (*nervously*) Perhaps we'd better get down there. Paul will be waiting.
Sarah How did he seem? What's your impression?
June He seemed rather pale.
Sarah I don't think he should take the service next Sunday.
June There is the Reverend Nicholson ...
Sarah A woman? (*She shrugs*) I'm afraid my husband leans towards St Paul in these matters — that women should remain silent in church.
June Isn't that rather old-fashioned?
Sarah Paul says the church should be old-fashioned — that's its strength. Besides, there's something else. We understand she may have a certain ... preference ...

Frank gives June a sly smile

Frank Preference?
Sarah There's a question mark ... That won't suit Paul. I think we'll have to go with the curate.

Frank nods solemnly

Frank Well, if there's a question mark ...
June (*hurriedly*) I think we should go ...
Sarah Will you be coming, Frank?
June No, Frank has to rest.
Frank I think I'll rest in the garden ...
June You didn't want to go in the garden.
Frank I do now. Perhaps I could sit on that bench out there ...

June looks out

June There's someone sitting there. You know how you hate sharing a bench.
Frank Someone sitting there? Are you sure?

Sarah looks out nervously

June Yes.
Frank I didn't see them. As if I haven't enough problems — glaucoma!

Sarah has fallen back and is clutching her throat

June What is it, Sarah?
Sarah It's that woman. She's here! I thought we'd seen the last of her.
June Who is she?
Sarah Tracey. I don't know her other name. I never thought she'd follow him here. She's obsessed.
June Obsessed?
Sarah With the vicar. Paul met her when he was at the cathedral.
Frank And she became obsessed?
Sarah It happens sometimes. Paul was giving her spiritual comfort during a bereavement. She was suicidal. She began to depend on him, taking up more and more of his time. She was exhausting him and he's not a well man ...

Sarah's voice dies away as she becomes aware of Frank's avid interest

Of course, this is strictly *entre nous* ...
Frank (*meekly*) Of course.

Sarah One of our reasons for coming here was to avoid this sort of strain. I never thought she'd follow. I thought she'd find someone else to cling to.

June She must be very disturbed.

Sarah She climbed the tower and threatened to throw herself into the churchyard.

Frank That tower's the third highest in the country — they wouldn't have had to dig a hole for her.

Sarah And Paul had to follow, pleading with her, in his condition, defibrillating all the way. It's because of her that he started smoking. He never smoked before. What with her and the heavy medication he's become a changed man.

Frank (*curiously*) In what way?

June gives him a sharp glance

Sarah I heard him swear the other day — in church. It was under his breath but I heard him.

Frank What did he say?

Sarah I've never heard him swear before. It was when his gaze fell on the collection — he was about to give the blessing when he observed the paltry sum and I saw his lips frame the words "bloody hell". He was never like this. Even when he fell down the steps of the crypt and broke his arm all he shouted out was "Sugar!"

Frank (*grinning*) Sugar! He's been keeping bad company.

June But he only framed the words, Sarah.

Sarah Even so — I reproached him with it. I said was it a proper thing for a man of the cloth to say in the house of Our Lord — even under his breath?

June What did he say?

Sarah I couldn't believe my ears. I can hardly bring myself to repeat it.

Frank As bad as that?

Sarah He said "Up yours." (*She takes a second glance outside*) I must find Paul and warn him.

Sarah exits hurriedly

Frank Tut-tut. Swearing in church.

June That's the effects of the medication. Look what it did to you.

Frank What did it do to me?

June You hallucinated.

Frank I didn't hallucinate. I had this feeling that something was creeping up behind me — it turned out to be you.

June Me? Bright green with pointed ears? That wasn't me, Frank.

Frank All right, it may be the medication but that's just releasing his inhibitions. What we're seeing is the real Reverend Latimer. You see, I know something you don't.

June And what's that?

Frank He's got something that belongs to that woman. She's prepared to share it but he won't. Who does that remind you of? Your previous incumbent — he of the discarded cassock.

June How do you know this?

Frank She told me.

June You've met her! You knew she was there. You wanted Sarah to know. Why? What are you trying to prove?

Frank I wanted to open your eyes. Your trouble is you can't see beyond that clerical collar. Oh, he looks the part, but so does an Elvis Presley look-alike — it's when they open their mouths ——

Paul enters from the hall

Paul Have you seen Sarah?

June (*quickly*) She was looking for you. You must have missed her.

Paul I was in my room ... (*He turns to the door*)

Frank She wanted to warn you ——

Paul (*turning*) Warn me?

Frank She's out there. On the bench.

Paul Who?

Frank Tracey.

Paul looks out

Paul (*under his breath*) Bugger!

Paul hurries from the room

June What did he say?

Frank Well, it wasn't sugar ...

CURTAIN

SCENE 2

The same. An hour later

The evening shadows are lengthening. The lights have been switched on. Frank is adjusting the crutches. Satisfied, he hoists himself up and crosses the room. Now he finds they are both too short and he's almost on his knees

June enters from the hall and looks down at him in amusement

June Well, if it isn't Tiny Tim.
Frank (*scowling*) Very funny. (*He returns to his chair throwing the crutches aside. He hoists one leg on to the coffee table*)

June puts the crutches against the wall

June There's a one-legged man looking for these.

Frank doesn't smile

Frank Get me a cushion.
June What's the magic word?
Frank Abracadabra.
June You know what I mean.
Frank (*through clenched teeth*) Please.

June makes Frank comfortable

You've been a long time.
June It didn't seem long.
Frank Was he ... charismatic?
June Yes. You should have been there. You should have seen those old people come alive.
Frank How could you tell? Did they open their eyes?
June They were enthralled. He was simple and direct.
Frank He was simple and direct in here — when he saw Tracey. And he used a magic word ...
June I didn't hear him.
Frank I did. It was under his breath but I heard. It sounded like sugar but it wasn't.
June Are you making a study of him?
Frank He's going to the dogs.

June I wish you weren't so cynical. You won't get better whilst you're like this.

Frank What's cynicism got to do with it?

June It's poisoning your system.

Frank I thought cynicism was supposed to be healthy. Anyway, believers get just as sick. Look at the vicar — belief didn't keep him healthy — that's if he does believe. What did he take as his text tonight? "Thou shalt not covert thy neighbours' furniture"?

June As a matter of fact it was the importance of marriage in modern society and the need for a moral compass. (*She looks pointedly at Frank*)

Frank That's rich — and Tracey still out there ...

June Oh, Lord. Is she? (*She crosses to the door and looks out*)

Frank She's been pacing about like Anna Karenina — waiting for Count Vronsky.

June Anna Karenina?

Frank She was suicidal — threw herself in front of a train.

June Honestly!

Frank Her presence hardly goes with the importance of marriage in modern society, does it?

June I wish you'd stop gloating.

Frank What else have I got to do? I live in a four-foot-six world full of grown ups. Everyone towers over me. All I can do is watch.

June You should have been there tonight. If you had been you wouldn't talk like this.

Frank That sermon may have gone down with those old boilers but I can see through him. What happened when he got Tracey to the top of that tower? He didn't read to her from the Corinthians. He probably had a leg over.

June After all those steps? Before he went into hospital he could barely climb into the pulpit.

Frank That was before. He's got his second wind now.

June He prayed for you tonight.

Frank looks shocked

Frank He did what?

June He prayed for you.

Frank How do you know?

June I was there.

Frank You mean, you heard him?

June Everyone did.

Frank In front of everyone?

June Yes.

Frank What must they think?

June They prayed too.

Frank For me?

June Yes.

Frank I'm not having that.

June Not much you can do about it.

Frank Now I've got total strangers praying for my recovery!

June They didn't pray for your recovery.

Frank They didn't?

June They prayed for God to give you strength.

Frank They're expecting the worst then?

June Strength to face your ordeal.

Frank No mention of a cure?

June Paul feels that we shouldn't ask God for favours.

Frank Well, it would have been worth a try. Not that I believe in it.

June You could hardly ask God for a favour, could you?

Frank You do think it's a punishment, don't you? You still haven't forgiven me.

June I've forgiven you, Cockie, but you can't expect me to forget. I haven't got amnesia.

Frank If you can't forget how can you forgive me?

June I remember without malice.

Frank But you have forgiven me?

June Yes. It's my Christian duty.

Frank All of them?

June Yes. (*Pause*) How many were there?

Frank I was on the road for years. I was lonely.

June Not for long.

Frank But you have forgiven me.

June You mean for the ones you told me about, the ones I found out about, or the ones I don't know about?

Frank I've told you everything.

June Then I've forgiven you for everything.

Frank I wouldn't do it now.

June Frank! You couldn't do it now! You're in a wheelchair.

Frank I wouldn't if I could. You don't know what it was like. Those long nights on the road. Those lonely nights in hotel rooms — the mini-bar reduced to a slimline tonic — laughter from downstairs.

June And what about me? Alone in an empty house — the level in the sherry decanter getting lower and lower — so bored I was ready to hurl myself through the double glazing.

Frank Ah, but you had your religion to sustain you. You had God.

June It wasn't God's low opinion that worried me, Frank — it was yours.

Frank Mine!
June Why are you surprised? (*Sadly*) We both know I loved you more than you loved me. In fact you counted on it.

Paul enters. He crosses to retrieve his scarf and coat and puts them on

Paul Sorry to disturb you ... (*He looks out into the garden and his voice dies away*)
Frank Going out?
Paul I thought I'd take a stroll.
Frank She's still out there.
Paul I know. (*Sighing*) I suppose I'll have to see her.
Frank She seems to think you have something that belongs to her.
Paul That's not true. She's disturbed, the effect of her bereavement. What you see out there is an error of judgement.
June Frank thought it was Anna Karenina.
Paul I shouldn't have got involved.
Frank Why did you?
Paul It was a mistake. I was recently out of hospital. I wasn't thinking clearly. The medication, I suppose. I should have referred her to a psychiatrist.
Frank Then you don't believe in the power of prayer?
Paul Prayer alone won't cure a sick mind any more than it can mend a broken leg, all we can do is ——
Frank Pray for strength?
Paul Yes. But she needs help and I can't give it to her. She began to interrupt the service. The Bishop thought it better if I faded from the scene for a while.
June You really shouldn't put yourself through this, Paul.
Paul I have to.
June Then wrap up well, there's a chill in the air.
Paul (*smiling*) I will.
June Make sure you do. (*She fusses over his scarf*)

Frank watches him jealously

Frank What was wrong with you?
Paul Nothing now. It's the tablets.
Frank (*studying him*) Did you have anything to do with diesel oil?
Paul (*staring*) What? No!
June Frank, what a stupid question.
Paul Why did you ask that?
Frank (*awkwardly*) Well, I ... er ... I read somewhere that exposure to fumes from diesel oil can cause ... What was wrong with you?

Paul Heart.

Frank Can cause heart trouble.

June It must have been very serious.

Paul I was given six months to live.

June Were they certain?

Paul Oh, yes. Medicine's come a long way — they can now tell us when we're going to die — they can't always stop it.

Frank But they did — in your case.

Paul Did they?

June (concerned) Don't say you're going to die, Paul.

Paul Well, let's say, I'm not boasting of tomorrow.

Frank Neither am I. I was playing tennis ——

June Frank, we know — but we're talking about something a little more serious.

Frank Serious!

June Was it a bypass?

Paul No.

Frank That's the serious one.

Paul This was serious. One in a million, Frank ...

Frank One in a million!

June Then I don't know why you're so reticent. Frank would have taken out advertising.

Frank What!

Paul I suppose I didn't want my flock to think I'm an invalid. It's something I can't get used to. I've always been extremely active.

Frank So have I. I was playing ——

June The heart's never been Frank's problem — it's proved very robust.

Frank Well, it looks as if there's a divine hand at work here. They said you were going to die — and you didn't.

Paul No, but someone did. They had to.

Frank and June stare at each other

June What do you mean?

Paul I had a transplant.

Frank You mean you've got someone's heart in there?

Paul I like to think of it as mine now.

Frank My God!

June Frank.

Frank Doesn't it feel strange?

Paul Not really.

Frank It would feel strange to me. Very strange.

Paul It's only a muscle.

Frank It may be a muscle to you — it was life and death to him.

Paul I don't like to dwell on it.

Frank I don't blame you. I wouldn't like to dwell on it. Someone's heart beating for me.

Paul (*tersely*) It's my heart now.

Frank Where did it come from? That's what I'd want to know.

Paul You're not told that. It's an anonymous gift. Someone killed in an accident — fortunately with a donor card.

Frank Fortunate for you.

Paul Yes.

Frank God moves in mysterious ways ...

June He still has work for you, Paul.

Frank Don't you mean for both of them? I can understand your reticence, Paul.

Paul Why?

Frank Some people, church people, may think that you're clinging rather tenaciously to life when you could have gone to the peace everlasting.

Paul I feel there is work to be done.

Frank And what happens when you get to heaven and meet your donor looking for his heart? Or doesn't the church have a position on this?

Paul I believe we're changed in form and substance.

Frank Oh, you mean we'll all float around like little sunbeams. Is that it, Vicar? Do you subscribe to the sunbeam theory?

Paul I don't know.

June begins to assemble the wheelchair

Frank We had a travel agent like you once. He didn't know. We finished up in a room facing the cement works.

Paul There are many mysteries, Frank.

Frank Yes, and here's one. When you went on the waiting list, did you pray for a heart?

Paul If it was God's wish.

Frank So you were both in on it. You were praying for someone's death.

Paul I didn't think of it like that.

Frank I'm sure you didn't.

Frank finds himself being assisted by June into the wheelchair

What are you doing?

June I'm taking you round the roses.

Frank I don't want to go round the roses.
June You did an hour ago.
Frank I've changed my mind.
June Too late. (*She begins to push him out into the garden*)

Frank looks back

Frank You're in luck, Paul. She's gone.

   They exit into the garden

Paul looks after them. Satisfied, he begins to remove scarf and coat

   Sarah enters with a half-empty bottle of vodka and a handbag

Paul (*guiltily*) Ah, there you are.

Sarah regards him coldly

   Where have you been?
Sarah I've been to your room — tidying up. (*She places the bottle on the table*) More side effects? Why?
Paul You know why.
Sarah No — tell me.
Paul (*desperately*) I have to feed him, Sarah.
Sarah Do you realize what you're saying?
Paul Yes.
Sarah You tell everyone it's just a muscle and you talk to me as if it's a person. (*She holds up bottle*) This will kill you.
Paul If I don't feed him he'll kill me.
Sarah How?
Paul He'll reject me.
Sarah I see. Is that what you're doing — making him welcome? Smoking and drinking. How do you know he needs this?
Paul I can feel it.
Sarah You can feel it?
Paul I can feel the craving ...
Sarah And were you feeding this craving the other night?
Paul (*frowning*) The other night?
Sarah The last night we slept together. When you leapt on me.
Paul Leapt on you?
Sarah Yes, Leapt on me.
Paul I don't remember any leaping.
Sarah Leaping and shouting.

Paul Shouting? I don't remember shouting.

Sarah You don't remember much do you? My only comfort was that the children were away at school — although they could have probably heard you in Kent.

Paul What did I shout?

Sarah At first: "Come on, come on."

Paul "Come on. Come on"?

Sarah Several times. As if we were late for an appointment.

Paul I must have been dreaming.

Sarah You weren't dreaming. I may be a vicar's wife but I knew where we were going. Then it was: "Take that, and that — and that."

Paul Take that?

Sarah This went on for some time. Then it was: "Yes. Yes. Yes."

Paul Why was I shouting yes?

Sarah I thought you could tell me. It wasn't a response to anything I'd said. I could barely get my breath. It seemed to be an expression of satisfaction. Whether it came from you or your friend within your breast, I'm not sure. Don't you remember any of this?

Paul I remember waking up. You were taking my pulse.

Sarah I was concerned that you may have gone out of rhythm. I was reaching for your tablets when you rolled over, punched the air with your fist, gave a shout of triumph, and fell asleep.

Paul Did I do all that?

Sarah It doesn't say much for you or your friend. (*Pause*) That's if he is to blame ...

Paul What do you mean?

Sarah When did all this start, Paul?

Paul When I had the heart.

Sarah No, it started when you met that girl. She's been the influence. Everyone's noticed the change in you. Even the Bishop. He saw you at the gala eating a burger and drinking from a can of lager. His glance was withering. And later when he saw you walking around the stalls eating peanuts.

Paul What's wrong with eating peanuts?

Sarah You weren't just eating them. You were throwing them in the air and catching them in your mouth. (*Pause*) Who were you making love to that last night, Paul?

Paul (*frowning*) It must have been you.

Sarah Must have been! There was a time when it was definitely me. When you loved your Moppet. When you loved me with all your heart.

Paul Yes. You had my heart, Sarah. But it's gone. It was worn out. This one isn't mine — and it isn't yours.

He exits into the hall

Sarah chokes back a sob. She is about to follow when she remembers the bottle. She returns and slips it into her bag

As she does so, June enters

June I've left him among the roses.
Sarah (*controlling herself*) Does he like roses?
June No. He's furious. He says the pollen gets up his nose. He hates being left in a wheelchair. He says it's abuse. But I have to get away sometimes.
Sarah I know what you mean.
June They're like children.
Sarah I know. Now he wants to ride around the parish on a motorbike! He doesn't even have a licence. He can barely ride a bicycle! (*Pause*) But there's something else. (*She dabs her nose and sniffs*)
June What is it, Sarah?
Sarah (*after a pause*) This is strictly *entre nous*.
June Of course.
Sarah I'm sure it must be the medication.
June What is?
Sarah I'm not a typical vicar's wife, June. I've seen something of life. When I was young, much younger, I went wild in Tuscany.
June Tuscany?
Sarah More than once — twice in fact. Of course that was before I met Paul.
June Of course.
Sarah So I am prepared for most things. But since Paul is not a well man ... I didn't expect ... what happened.
June What happened?
Sarah I think it must be some sort of side effect. And I wondered if the drugs had affected Frank in the same way ...
June What way?
Sarah (*lowering her voice*) Sexually.
June No. (*Sadly*) They just make him sleepy.
Sarah I wish they made Paul sleepy.
June Sarah, what did happen?
Sarah Well, it wasn't the normal warm affection between man and wife. He was like a stranger — a stranger with erotic impulses. He leapt on me whooping.
June Whooping?
Sarah And shouting. "Come on. Come on." And then. "Take that — and that, and that".

June Take that?

Sarah "And that, and that, and that".

June That — meaning?

Sarah Yes.

June This went on for some time?

Sarah It was interminable. I said, "Steady on, Paul". But he didn't appear to hear me. Just "take that, and that, and that." I'm surprised he didn't tie me to the bedpost and lash me with a whip. Then suddenly, it was, "Yes! Yes! Yes!" And it was all over — bar the shouting.

June And you think it was the drugs?

Sarah What else?

June (*thoughtfully*) Any particular one?

Sarah I've no idea.

June Not the sort you'd get over the counter, I suppose ...?

Sarah Hardly. (*Pause*) When I say he was a different person — perhaps he thought I was.

June A different person? What do you mean?

Sarah I often saw them around the Close. Their heads bent in deep conversation. I know he was consoling her in her bereavement, but ——

June You mean Tracey?

Sarah She's very attractive.

June So are you.

Sarah Do you think so?

June Yes.

Sarah I am considered rather chic — for a vicar's wife.

June You are chic.

Sarah I have this cocktail dress — I don't think you've seen it. It does draw the eye. Paul's very fond of it.

June Sarah, wear it when you come tomorrow. Don't wait for cocktails.

Sarah So you do think she's more attractive.

June No but ——. Did he give you any reason to think this? Did he mention her name?

Sarah No. He did mutter a name before he fell asleep but it wasn't Tracey. It was a man's.

June What!

Sarah It was Gerald, or Gordon somebody, or Graham. I didn't quite catch it.

June Did you ask him about it?

Sarah He'd fallen asleep. Besides, I thought it might be an extra complication. It could confuse him further.

June Confuse him?

Sarah Has he mentioned his transplant?

June Yes.

Sarah Well, he feels that the donor may be having a malign influence on him. I know it's ridiculous ——

June Or he could be simply using a man's name as a cover. I've known it happen. They call them Fred or Bill, names like that.

Sarah Why?

June In case they talk in their sleep.

Sarah Fred or Bill?

June Or even Gerald or Gordon.

Sarah (*studying June*) You're very wise in these matters, aren't you, June?

June I've had to be.

Sarah I'd better go and collect the prayer books ...

June I'll help you.

Sarah What about Frank?

June I'll pop back for him.

They cross to the hall door

Oh, Sarah, when he says "come on — come on"...

Sarah I should follow?

June No — get there before him.

They exit

Frank's voice can be heard from the garden

Frank (*off*) It's all clear — they've gone ...

Frank enters from the garden in the wheelchair. He is being pushed by Tracey

Tracey I shouldn't be in here. But I didn't like to see you stranded.

Frank (*darkly*) It wouldn't be the first time. She left me outside a butcher's shop once for two hours whilst she had tea with her sister. Said she forgot about me. Two hours! I could have been turned into a string of sausages for all she cared. One day she's going to leave me on a steep slope with the handbrake off and her problems will be solved.

Tracey I don't believe that. I saw her with you. I could see she cared. I wish I had someone to care for like that ...

Frank I'm sorry — that was thoughtless of me. I'd forgotten about your loss. I told the vicar you were here.

Tracey He doesn't want to see me, does he?

Frank That's because he has something that belongs to you. Isn't that it?

Tracey prowls around the room inhaling deeply

Tracey He's been back here.
Frank Diesel oil?
Tracey And candy floss.
Frank Candy floss?
Tracey The smell of the fairground.
Frank (*staring*) The vicar smells of the fairground.
Tracey Not the vicar — Melvin.
Frank Who's Melvin?
Tracey He was my lover. He's dead.
Frank And he left something to the vicar?
Tracey Yes. His heart.
Frank His heart!
Tracey He left a donor card.
Frank But that's confidential. How do you know the vicar's got his heart?
Tracey My sister works at the hospital. She knows about these things. We followed it. As soon as his heart hit the bucket we were off. Lights flashing, sirens screaming. We followed it to the hospital. The recipient was the Reverend Paul Latimer. The liver and kidney went elsewhere — they didn't interest me. But the heart ...
Frank Is that why you followed him here?
Tracey I have to be close to it.
Frank Why?
Tracey It still beats for me.
Frank How do you know?
Tracey I've felt it.
Frank You have?
Tracey It goes faster when I put my hand on it.
Frank You've put your hand on it?
Tracey Yes. I've felt it pulsing and throbbing.
Frank Inside the vicar?
Tracey Yes.
Frank Did he mind?
Tracey What?
Frank That you put your hand on it?
Tracey He said if it gave me comfort ... It was Melvin — I could feel it.
Frank And whilst Melvin was pulsing and throbbing what was the vicar doing?

Tracey I suppose he was pulsing and throbbing too — he couldn't help it, could he?

Frank I suppose not.

Tracey They're inseparable — that's what pleases me.

Frank Why?

Tracey I loved Melvin but he was a bit of a bastard and he wasn't getting any better. When I found out where his heart had gone, as you can imagine, I was thrilled.

Frank Thrilled?

Tracey It had gone to a vicar. I mean it's such an improvement.

Frank The vicar thinks it's only a muscle.

Tracey I don't. When Melvin signed that donor card do you know what he said? "You won't get rid of me that easy, Trace. I'll be back." And he is — in the flesh.

Frank In the Reverend Latimer's flesh.

Tracey Yes.

Frank Why did you climb the tower? The third tallest in England. One hundred and sixty-five steps. The only people you meet are steeplejacks and suicides.

Tracey I wasn't suicidal. It was so that we wouldn't be disturbed.

Frank Why?

Tracey He didn't come on to me, if that's what you're thinking. His palms were sweating but that was the climb.

Frank What about Melvin? Did he come on to you?

Tracey Melvin couldn't stand heights. He had giddy spells — that was the trouble.

Frank Trouble?

Tracey He was a wall of death rider.

Frank What?

Tracey At the fair.

Frank The vicar has the heart of a wall of death rider?

Tracey That's where we met — at the fair. I told fortunes. He came to me to have his cards read. He was worried about the giddy spells and going over the edge. I was able to reassure him.

Frank Reassure him?

Tracey That things would turn out all right.

Frank (*after a pause*) He's dead.

Tracey Yes — he did go over the edge — landed in the car park. His last words were, "Oh, shit." Hardly dignified.

Frank But you said things would turn out all right.

Tracey They did. Look where he ended up.

Frank In the car park.

Tracey No. You don't get it do you? Melvin never led a good life. Even his death was bizarre. Now it has dignity. He's going to heaven with the Reverend Latimer. How lucky can you get?

Frank considers this for a moment

Frank If he is lucky ...
Tracey What do you mean?
Frank How do you know that the vicar's going to heaven?
Tracey Of course he is. He's a man of the cloth.
Frank The cloth's a little threadbare these days, Tracey. And don't forget those sweating palms ...
Tracey What are you getting at?
Frank That the vicar may be doing some pulsing and throbbing on his own account.
Tracey No, I'd know Melvin's heartbeat anywhere.
Frank Then perhaps Melvin's trying to tell you something.
Tracey What?
Frank That he's trapped. That he wants to be free, free of the Reverend Latimer. Free of all his hypocrisy. And only you can free him.
Tracey How?
Frank I think you know how ...

There are sounds from the hall. Tracey moves towards the garden. Frank catches her arm

Don't go.

Paul enters

Paul Oh. I thought you'd gone. Why must you keep following me?
Tracey I'm not following you — I'm following Melvin.
Paul He's dead! I don't know where he is now but he's not here! All we have left is a piece of meat.
Tracey I know Melvin didn't have a sparkling personality but he's more than a piece of meat. And don't forget that part of him is keeping you alive.
Paul I know — and don't think I'm not grateful. And I'm sure this selfless act has given him eternal life. But he's simply not here.
Tracey Then why can I smell diesel oil and candy floss?
Paul It's all in your mind.
Tracey You didn't say that on our walks together. Remember how he spoke through you? The things he said? "Let him kiss me with the kisses of his mouth."

Paul I was speaking for Melvin. I was endeavouring to show that the bible ...

He breaks off as he becomes aware of Frank's avid interest

Would you excuse us, Frank?
Frank Don't mind me.
Paul This is rather personal ..

He wheels Frank to the door. Frank catches hold of the small table and drags it with him. Paul detaches him from it

Just for a moment.

Frank catches hold of the door frame

Frank Don't worry — you won't shock me ...
Paul This won't take a moment.

Paul manages to evict Frank

Frank exits

Paul closes the door. He and Tracey face each other

(*Uneasily*) I was merely trying to show that the bible doesn't condemn physical love — love that meant so much to you and Melvin ...

His voice dies away as he finds himself cornered by Tracey

Tracey (*huskily*) "Let him kiss me with the kisses of his mouth for his love is sweeter than wine. Stay me with flagons — comfort me with apples — for I'm sick with love."

She kisses Paul long and earnestly. Paul stands back and stares at her in amazement

Paul (*broad cockney*) Gordon Bennett!

END OF ACT I

ACT II

SCENE 1

The visitors' room. The following evening

Frank is alone at the coffee table reading a paper. There is the sound of a motor horn from the hall. Frank stares at the door

June enters on a small motorized buggy. She smiles at Frank and pips the horn. Frank returns to his paper

June puts the buggy through its paces. She circles Frank, advancing and reversing and spinning around, ending with a final pip in front of Frank. Frank lowers his paper

Frank I can't help observing that you appear to be in charge of a small motorized vehicle.

June It's a buggy.

Frank Is it?

June I want you to try it.

Frank Why?

June It'll make you more mobile.

Frank Not for long. If I take that on the road I'll be squashed like a fly.

June No — it's for the house. You can whizz round the furniture in this.

Frank If I try whizzing around the furniture in that I'll finish up in the fireplace.

June How do you know?

Frank Because I can't turn my neck. You've seen me trying to park a car.

June Well, that problem's solved.

Frank What do you mean?

June I've got an invalid permit! We can park anywhere now. Invalid spaces, yellow lines — even double yellow lines. They're changing hands for ten thousand pounds in London. So you see there are advantages ... (*Her voice dies away*)

Frank Yes — and if I lose any more weight I'll be able to get into my old suits. Every cloud has a silver lining. (*Pause*) My voice is getting higher.

June It's not getting higher.

Frank It is in the mornings.

June It's the same as it's always been.

Frank It's the steroids.

June It's not the steroids.

Frank It's piping.

June It's not piping.

Frank It's getting higher.

June It's not getting higher.

Frank One day it'll only be audible to dogs. It's almost a treble.

June It's not a treble.

Frank I'll have a higher voice than you've got.

June Frank, your voice is just the same.

Frank You mean it's always been high.

June No! (*She puts the buggy to one side*) I'll leave it here. You may change your mind. (*She hands him a tablet dispenser*) Here are your tablets. I'm going to have a word with matron about them. (*Worried*) Apparently no one else should touch them.

Frank Why?

June I'm not sure ...

June exits

Frank looks anxious for a moment and then checks the dispenser

Paul enters. He nods a greeting

Paul Frank.

Frank gives him a brief nod. Paul senses a coolness and sits on the far side of the room. Frank stretches for the thermos jug which is a little out of reach. Paul watches anxiously

Can I get that?

Frank I can manage. (*He stretches his hand out further. The jug remains tantalizingly out of reach*)

Paul contorts his body in sympathy. Frank overbalances and falls out of his chair. Paul leaps to his feet

Paul Can I help?
Frank Don't bother. (*He struggles back into his chair*)
Paul Should I ring the bell?
Frank No.

Frank pulls the coffee table closer. Paul puts a hand on his brow and bows his head. Frank observes this

(*Sourly*) Have you got a headache?
Paul No.
Frank You did that at dinner.
Paul Did I?
Frank After those three glasses of wine. Were you praying?
Paul Do you mind?
Frank I prefer that you did it in your own time. And made it a little less obvious.
Paul Why? "If the trumpet sounds an uncertain note who shall prepare himself for battle?"
Frank Not me. If you're praying for me — don't.
Paul I forgot — you don't believe in prayer.
Frank I prefer steroids.
Paul (*smiling*) It goes well with steroids.
Frank No, I'm immune. I've been exposed too long. Aunt Marion in South Africa has been pulling out all the stops. She even climbed Table Mountain to get closer. June and the sewing circle have been wearing their knees out for me. Her mother's even buried the hatchet and joined in. And now there's you. And you saw the result. I went down on that floor like a roll of lino. If you're going to pray — pray for yourself. You may need it.
Paul What do you mean?
Frank I'm not sure what happened in here last night after I'd been evicted but she didn't give you the kiss of peace — war is about to break out when she meets your wife. The trumpet had better not sound an uncertain note then. She's back.
Paul Where?
Frank On the bench.

Paul looks out. He closes the curtains

Paul She's deluded.
Frank She doesn't appear deluded to me.
Paul She doesn't realize that it's the brain that governs the emotions — not the heart.

Frank Is it? They don't send a brain with an arrow through it on St Valentine's Day — they send a heart.

Paul That's an old-fashioned belief.

Frank According to you the church is old-fashioned — that's its strength.

Paul Melvin's dead — that's not a belief, that's a fact.

Frank (*slyly*) Is it? Then why do I detect the faint aroma of diesel oil and candy floss?

Paul (*staring*) What?

Frank Do you know something? I don't think Melvin's keeping you alive — I think you're keeping him alive.

Paul Nonsense.

Frank Is it? That the heart doesn't feel emotion? Then why do you tell your congregation to follow their hearts? You don't ask them to follow their brains — that's for cynics like me. Is that what you were doing last night — following your heart? Well, it couldn't have been the old one, could it?

Paul (*frowning, he sniffs*) Diesel oil?

Frank And candy floss. A philosopher once said, "All the knowledge I possess anyone can acquire but my heart is my own ..."

Paul What?

Frank Not that yours is your own exactly ...

June and Sarah enter

Sarah is wearing the slinky cocktail dress which she tends to fuss with

Sarah Bit of a prob, Sausage.

Paul winces at the appellation

Paul What?

Sarah The curate can't take the service on Sunday.

Paul Why not?

Sarah He's been apprehended in a gents' loo. He said he was asking directions but the police thought otherwise, last night being the fifth time this week.

Frank So the curate has preferences?

Sarah That leaves us with the Reverend Nicholson.

Paul No, I don't think so.

June She's very well-liked.

Paul She has no confidence.

June Well, she won't have unless she's allowed ——

Paul I'll give the sermon ... (*He turns to the door*)

Sarah Where are you going?
Paul I thought I'd take a shower..
Sarah I'll come with you.
Paul Is that necessary?
Sarah You shouldn't have a shower unattended.
Paul Shouldn't I?
Sarah Paul, you've reached a stage in life, a stage which most men reach eventually, when they must never lock the bathroom door.

Sarah follows Paul out of the room

June (*frowning*) I wish he'd give her a chance.
Frank He doesn't approve of women priests, does he?
June No.
Frank But you do.
June Paul has his views — I have mine.
Frank (*grinning*) Do I detect a schism?
June A great many priests are like that. You won't turn me against him.
Frank That girl's back.
June Oh, no! (*She looks out*) She must be stalking him.
Frank Or Melvin ...
June (*staring*) Who's Melvin?
Frank Tracey's boyfriend. Or should I say ex-boyfriend? I'm never quite sure.
June Melvin? (*Looking out again*) Has he come as well?
Frank Yes.
June What's he doing here?
Frank Nothing. He's dead.
June If he's dead — how can he be here?
Frank Because he's still pulsing and throbbing.
June He can't be pulsing and throbbing and dead.
Frank He can — that's the trouble. If the vicar's pulsing and throbbing, so is Melvin.
June Would you stop talking in riddles?
Frank Let me put it in a nutshell. Paul has Melvin's heart — or Melvin has Paul's body. I'm not sure which. Neither is Tracey. The vicar's not too sure either. It's a battle.

June stares at him in astonishment

June You call that a nutshell?
Frank I'm getting there. You see after Melvin came off the wall of death ——

June Wall of what?

Frank Death. Aptly named as it turned out. Too near the edge. Car park. They found a donor card — and the vicar got Melvin's heart. Now Tracey's come here to claim it.

June The vicar's transplant!

Frank Yes.

June But how would they know? It's confidential. It's carried out in total secrecy.

Frank Not total. Not according to Tracey's sister. She's in the know. They were after it as soon as it hit the bucket.

June So that's it! That's the hold she has over Paul. The heart transplant. That's why he's been so reticent. He hasn't even told Sarah.

Paul There's a lot of things he hasn't told Sarah. They were alone in here last night.

June What?

Frank You didn't know that, did you? I was bundled out of this room. Bundled — into the hall. So that they could be alone.

June What were they doing?

Frank He'd tell you he was counselling her but I think he'd seen the twin peaks of Sheba ...

June Don't start that again, Frank. I can't follow you.

Frank He swears, he drinks, he smokes. What else is left? Hm?

June I don't want to hear any more.

Frank It does shake your faith a little, doesn't it?

June No. You've always confused the message with the messenger, Frank. Suppose he is all you say — that doesn't affect the message he brings.

Frank Messages are for the Royal Mail.

June I don't want you to say any more about this, Frank — not to anyone — certainly not to Sarah.

Frank You mean that the vicar has a preference?

June If you do — I'll take you out in that wheelchair and leave you on the M1 — fast lane.

Frank You'd do that to a cripple?

June Yes.

Frank Is that what you call solicitude?

June You've had enough solicitude. I thought you married a younger woman for love and affection in your old age. You didn't want love and affection. You wanted someone strong enough to push your wheelchair.

Frank Now, June, remember your vows, made in church, in front of witnesses. In sickness and in health. Remember what you promised — in front of God?

June I know what I promised.

Frank Well, now you've got the sickness.

June The health wasn't that hot either! But you're right, this is worse. You've turned into a mean, miserable toad.

Frank Toad? Not yet — I'm still a tadpole.

June I do everything for you. And all I hear is how much you hate the world. You look for faults in everyone. I remember how you'd follow the previous vicar into the newsagents in the hope you'd find him buying the *News of the World*.

Frank I don't remember that.

June Well, remember this. I put your socks on — your shoes on — I take you to the toilet — and if you talk about Paul to anyone — you'll find yourself sockless, shoeless and shitless!

June storms out into the corridor slamming the door

Frank (*calling after her*) You'd do that to a sick man? Am I to depend on the kindness of strangers — like Blanche du Bois?

Tracey's head appears around the garden door

Tracey I thought I heard your voice.

Frank (*sadly*) The voice is usually the last thing to go. Come in.

He watches her enter

I could skip over those steps a year ago — carrying my granddaughter — now she skips over them on her own and I can't even make it.

Tracey Is he about?

Frank The vicar? Tread warily. He's with his wife. And she means business — she's wearing her cocktail dress.

Tracey Not much chance of catching him on his own?

Frank Not at the moment. I believe he's having an assisted shower. She doesn't like to leave him. She thinks he's not long for this world.

Tracey (*sighing*) Why am I always attracted to men with a death wish?

Frank The vicar hasn't got a death wish. He's clinging to the wreckage. He's not quite ready for the promised land, not yet.

Tracey Even so, I saw black plumed horses when I came here tonight.

Frank You don't have to be psychic to see those. Have you checked the average age in that lounge?

Tracey I was thinking of the vicar. He's living on the edge. Why am I always drawn to men who live on the edge?

Frank Tracey, Melvin didn't live on the edge — he went over it, remember? And you said he'd be lucky.

Tracey He was, in a way. He won at bingo the night before.

Frank I don't think that would be any consolation.

Tracey (*sadly*) You're right. And it was all my fault.

Frank Your fault?

Tracey I pushed him too hard. He used to be on the hoop-la until they found the rings wouldn't go over the prizes. He was at a loose end when I met him. It was me who suggested the wall of death. He was always fond of motorbikes. If only I had known.

Frank I thought you were supposed to know. You tell fortunes.

Tracey I know but the future only goes so far — at least mine does.

Frank What happens to it?

Tracey It becomes the past. And then it's too late. Look at my past — widowed at twenty-five. Well, I would have been if I'd been married. I wish he'd stuck to the hoop-la. We could have had bigger rings. I blame myself. I suppose that's why I can't bear to lose him.

Frank If it is him. If it is Melvin.

Tracey That's what I have to find out. Who did I kiss last night? The vicar or Melvin? Whose palms were sweating? Were they Melvin's or the Reverend Latimer's?

Paul enters from the hall

Tracey inhales

I can smell diesel oil.

Paul You can't — I've had a shower.

Tracey corners him

Tracey You can't wash it away, Paul. Diesel oil and candy floss ...

Paul casts a nervous glance at Frank who has retired behind his newspaper. Paul moves to the far end of the room. Tracey follows

Can't you feel it? Can't you hear it? The throb of the generators, the wild music?

Paul (*hissing*) No.

Tracey The screams from the big wheel? The smell of diesel, of candy floss and toffee apples ...? Your life, Melvin.

Paul I'm not Melvin.

Paul attempts to break away. Tracey catches hold of his hand. She pulls him to her

Frank peers over his newspaper for a moment. Tracey's voice is low and intense

Tracey Your palms are sweating — just like Melvin's. I could do that to him. I only had to put my arms around him and tickle his neck and blow in his ear ... And do you know what would happen? He'd swallow. Do you know why he'd swallow? Because his throat was dry. He hated doing that because he felt it gave him away. It made him feel in my power ... Are you in my power?

Paul swallows audibly

Paul No.
Tracey You swallowed.

Frank lowers his paper again

Paul I'm the Reverend Latimer.
Tracey Then be the Reverend Latimer.

Frank raises his paper. Tracey glances towards it and kisses Paul. She speaks in a low voice as she edges him towards the garden. Frank turns the newspaper in their direction

Remember how we talked. How you told me about David and Bathsheba. And Samson and Delilah. And Salome. And all that begatting. I didn't know the bible could be such hot stuff ...

She stands at the door still holding Paul's hand

Come outside, Reverend Latimer. "It is a beautiful evening calm and free, the holy time is quiet as a nun ..." You see, I remembered ...

They drift into the garden

Frank throws down his newspaper. He is avid with curiosity and is eager to follow. He looks around. His walking frame isn't there. His wheelchair is collapsed. He struggles on to the buggy. He switches on the controls. He finds himself going backwards instead of forwards. He spins around the room crashing into furniture. Chairs and tables are sent flying

Frank finds himself sailing out backwards through the curtains and into the garden

There is a loud crash and a despairing cry from outside

June enters in a hurry from the hall. She surveys the wreckage in astonishment

She turns to see Frank crawling back into the room. She assists him to a chair

June (*tidying the room*) What happened?

Frank I was trying out the chair.

June Why did you go outside?

Frank I didn't choose to. It s got a mind of its own. But do you know what I saw?

June What?

Frank Tracey and the vicar. Cavorting.

June I don't believe it.

Frank You'd better. I don't know what the bishop will make of it.

June You won't say a word.

Frank Someone should. Unless you want Melvin giving the sermon on Sunday. You should have seen them. They were wrestling with each other.

June stares around the room

June Did they do all this?

Frank No, I did that. Trying to keep out the way.

June Couldn't you have stopped it?

Frank How? They're bigger than I am. They tower above me. I'm in a land of giants. I'm a child. I'm a eunuch — I see but I don't understand.

June You understand all right. You could see the drugs are affecting him — you knew she was a disturbed young woman. And you just stood by.

Frank How many times do I have to tell you — I can't stand. He can. He can stand. He can walk. And what does he choose — the primrose path of dalliance.

June That's what it is, isn't it? He can walk — he can do the things you can't — not anymore. So you sit and watch — Frank, the happy eunuch.

Frank Not happy. Why should I get involved? You already talk about me as if I'm not here.

June I don't.

Frank You do. "I'm taking him out into the garden — the fresh air will do him good." "No, he doesn't eat those." "Just one sugar — he's sweet enough." And all the time I'm sitting there with an idiotic grin on my face.
June (*staring*) Do I do that?
Frank Yes.

Sarah enters

Sarah Where's Paul? He seems to have given me the slip ...

There's an awkward silence

Frank He's out there.

June darts Frank a glance

June I think he went for a smoke ... (*She crosses to draw the curtains further*)
Sarah He didn't even mention my dress.
June He has a lot on his mind ...
Sarah He says I'm not to call him Sausage any more. I always called him Sausage and he called me Moppet. He says it's twee.
Frank Well, it is a bit ——

June gives him a silencing glance

Sarah I never found Moppet twee. Now he says it's silly. That's because of her. (*She produces the cigarette packet and waves it in front of them*) I have his cigarettes. He hasn't gone for a smoke. He's out there with her, isn't he?
June It's the drugs. (*Hopefully*) Side effects.
Sarah It's suicide. This will kill him. How can a man with an irregular heartbeat and water retention become involved with that flibbertigibbet?
Frank (*staring*) Flibbertigibbet?
Sarah That's what she is. Common and unstable. It wouldn't last a week — even if he lived that long ...

Tracey is standing at the door

They all become aware of her. There's a silence

Tracey What's a flibbertigibbet?

Sarah An empty and frivolous person.
Tracey Oh, I just wondered.
Sarah Where's my husband?
Tracey Out there.
Sarah He's collapsed! (*She moves forward*)
Tracey No, he's in great shape. He asked me to give you this ... (*She hands Sarah Paul's clerical collar*)

Tracey exits

Sarah stares at the collar and screams

Curtain

Scene 2

The visitors' room. The following day

Frank is alone. He is moving around in his chair in some discomfort. There is no sign of a wheelchair

He presses the bell impatiently. He rocks to and fro. He presses the bell again. He pulls himself up on his walking frame and struggles to the garden door. He opens the door and begins to unzip. Facing on to the garden he stops abruptly. He gives a sheepish wave

Frank Good morning ...

He looks about the room. We can follow his train of thought. He regards a bowl of flowers. He considers the thought and then dismisses it. He eyes the thermos jug, lifts the lid and studies the level. He pours the water from the jug on to the bowl of flowers. He turns to the wall and with anxious glances towards the hall and half hidden by curtains begins to relieve himself

Tracey enters from the garden

Tracey Hello.

A muttered exclamation from Frank. He zips up and turns

Frank I wish you'd stop doing that. (*He places the jug out of reach on the bookcase*) Why can't you use the front door like everyone else?

Tracey Because they don't want me here. I can sense hostility.

Frank Your psychic powers are improving.

Tracey Is she very upset?

Frank You heard her. She called you a flibbertigibbet. She doesn't use that term lightly. In fact I thought it had gone out of fashion but no, it came forth new minted. I think it's the cocktail dress that's gone out of fashion. It seems to have lost its allure. She was once considered chic in ecclesiastical circles.

Tracey studies him

Tracey You're very biting, aren't you?

Frank What?

Tracey Everything you say — very biting.

Frank (*uneasily*) I wouldn't say that.

Tracey I would. Is it because you're ill?

Frank No!

Tracey Are you in pain? That would explain it.

Frank I'm not in pain. There's nothing to explain. I have a very sunny nature. I am not biting. What do you want? I thought we'd seen the last of you.

Tracey I want you to pass on a message.

Frank A message? Who for?

Tracey Paul.

Frank Look, I've been told not to get involved. He'll be down in minute. He's getting a few things together. Can't it wait?

Tracey No. Because when he comes down I won't be here.

Frank Where will you be?

Tracey Tunbridge Wells.

Frank (*staring*) I thought you were leaving together.

Tracey That was before.

Frank Before what?

Tracey There's been a slip-up.

Frank What sort of a slip-up?

Tracey My sister's just rung me. She's been making further enquiries and there's been an unexpected development ...

Frank How unexpected?

Tracey We followed the wrong heart.

Frank What?

Tracey There were two hearts that night. We followed the wrong one. Melvin isn't here.

Frank Tracey, I may not be psychic but I think I know where he is —
Tunbridge Wells.

Tracey That's right.

Frank That's right! What about the diesel oil, and the candy floss, and
the toffee apples? What about the throb of the generators and the cries
from the Big Wheel?

Tracey I must have got carried away..

Frank That's no excuse. As a medium you leave a great deal to be
desired. You said Melvin was on his way to heaven and he finds
himself in Tunbridge Wells.

Tracey Tunbridge Wells is highly regarded.

Frank I've nothing against Tunbridge Wells but I've never heard
anyone suggest we go there when we die!

Tracey That's where Melvin's gone. I must go to him.

Frank Do you know where to find him?

Tracey Yes. He's inside a dentist.

Frank A dentist? Well, the pay's better.

Tracey I have to hurry. He's getting married on Saturday.

Frank Melvin?

Tracey The dentist.

Frank What about Melvin? Is he going to be best man?

Tracey Melvin hasn't got any choice in the matter. The dentist said
if he had a new heart he'd propose to the girl of his dreams, and she
accepted. She was Miss Tunbridge Wells.

Frank Sounds as if Melvin's in for a good time.

Tracey Not without me. That's why I must go at once. Before they
leave for the Seychelles.

Frank The Seychelles?

Tracey That's where they're going for their honeymoon.

Frank That's nice. Wait a minute. You're not thinking of going with
them? Not on their honeymoon. Three's a crowd, Tracey.

Tracey You mean four.

Frank I keep forgetting Melvin.

Tracey You don't think it's a good idea?

Frank I don't think they will.

Tracey I'll exercise discretion.

Frank Perhaps a chance meeting by the pool?

Tracey I'd thought of that. I've packed my bikini. My sister's booked
a provisional flight.

Frank It pays to be prepared.

Tracey Tell Paul I'm sorry.

Frank (*grinning*) It'll be a pleasure.

Tracey (*studying him*) I can see it now.

Frank What?

Tracey That sunny nature.

Frank One has to bear up under life's disappointments. And Paul's going to be disappointed. Now that Melvin's in Tunbridge Wells he'll have to do his own pulsing and throbbing.

Tracey Not quite ...

Frank gives Tracey an alert glance

Frank You know something.

Tracey He still has a heart ...

Frank You know whose it is.

Tracey That man is so lucky.

Frank Is he?

Tracey My sister backtracked. Guess where his heart came from. It came from a vicar!

Frank A vicar!

Tracey How's that for compatibility? A young vicar. It's just like computer dating.

Frank I knew it! Didn't I say? When it comes to pulsing and throbbing there's no one to match a repressed cleric. What was the cause of death — heart failure during congress — no it couldn't have been heart failure — shot by a jealous parishioner?

Tracey It was a traffic accident. I took down the details. The donor was the Reverend Frances Venables. Very well regarded.

Frank And young. Plenty of mileage there, Tracey. He'll get plenty of pulsing and throbbing there.

Tracey Not exactly ... (*She hesitates*) When I said it was like computer dating ...

Frank Yes?

Tracey It's Frances with an e ...

Frank stares uncomprehendingly for a moment

Frank An e? You mean it's a ...?

Tracey Woman.

Frank He has a woman's heart?

Tracey Yes.

Frank Will it be strong enough?

Tracey It was strong enough last night. Besides, she's a hockey player.

Frank A hockey player. They can be really tough. They often play without shin pads. (*He breaks into a broad grin*)

Tracey I can see it ever so clearly now.

Frank What?

Tracey Your sunny nature.

Frank I've just realized. He has a woman priest by his side and there's nothing he can do about it. (*He begins to laugh*)

Tracey I wouldn't mention it to Paul.

Frank No, of course not.

Tracey crosses to the door

Tracey And you will tell him I'm sorry..

Frank (*chuckling*) Oh, yes.

Tracey (*looking back*) I can see it now. It's really broken through.

Frank What has?

Tracey Your sunny nature . .

Tracey exits

Frank is still chuckling

June enters

June I was waiting for her to go. You sound pleased with yourself.

Frank Do I?

June Why are you laughing?

Frank She said something funny. What's the matter? You say I don't laugh enough.

June I didn't say that. I said you were miserable.

Frank Isn't that the same thing?

June No, you laugh, Frank, but only at other people. You can't laugh at yourself — consequently you can't take it when others laugh at you.

Frank Who's laughing at me?

June No one. They wouldn't dare.

Frank And who am I laughing at?

June I imagine it's Paul at the moment.

Frank Why not? He's a scream.

June If he's behaving badly just remember he's on heavy medication.

Frank The drugs have only revealed the dark side of his nature.

June We all have a dark side, Frank — look at yours.

Frank I seem to be getting a lot of character analysis at the moment.

June What did Tracey have to say?

Frank A great deal. Whoever's caused all this ... hurly-burly ... it's not Melvin. He's in Tunbridge Wells.

June What!

Frank Working in the Health Service — drilling teeth. Off to the Seychelles on Saturday.

June How do you know?

Frank Tracey's sister. There's been a slip-up. So you see, all this had nothing to do with Melvin.

June I never thought it did.

Frank (*staring*) You didn't?

June The whole thing was ridiculous. But the trouble was Paul believed it. He was drugged and vulnerable. He was open to suggestion.

Frank (*beaming*) Well, I have another suggestion for him. He has the heart of a vicar.

June (*sighing*) He did have once.

Frank He has now.

June (*surprised*) What?

Frank According to Tracey's sister.

June I'm getting a little tired of Tracey's sister.

Frank Don't be. She brings glad tidings of great joy. A young vicar had died and left Paul a legacy.

June You mean ... his heart? That's wonderful!

Frank Not *his* heart ... exactly.

June I don't understand.

Frank The donor is the Reverend Frances Venables ...

June Yes?

Frank Frances with an e ...

June You mean ...?

Frank (*nodding*) A woman.

June A woman? (*Pause*) Will it be strong enough?

Frank It's standing up pretty well at the moment. You know what this means?

June What?

Frank He's got his woman priest whether he likes it or not.

June Oh, dear. Poor Paul.

Frank What do you mean? Poor Paul? He's lucky to get it. He should be grateful. What's so special about him? He's no better than the rest of us, in fact he's worse. He was tempted and he fell — that's all there is to it.

June You were tempted and you fell.

Frank I'm not a man of the cloth.

June He's only fallen once.

Frank Once is enough.

June It wasn't for you.

Frank I knew you'd rake that up. You haven't forgiven me.

June I have.

Frank No, you say you've forgiven me but you haven't. And you're supposed to be a Christian. What do you really believe in? I'd love to know.

June (*after hesitating*) I believe Jesus was a good man ...

Frank Yes, and who killed him? The priests. And why didn't God save him? Because he doesn't exist.

June Doesn't he? Then how did he make the world?

Frank June, there are millions of planets out there ——

June Planets! Don't talk to me about planets. There's more life in our back garden. (*Scathingly*) They can't even grow weeds!

Frank June, there was a big bang — our whole world is made of gases.

June You mean you are — hot air. I know why you don't believe in God. It's because you can't bear the thought of someone being more important than you.

Frank (*sighing*) Why do all our arguments end in personal abuse?

June moves towards the door

Where are you going?

June To find Paul and tell him.

Frank I think he arranged to meet Tracey here.

June If I miss him — detain him until Sarah comes. She's bringing pictures of the children.

Frank Why? Doesn't he remember what they look like?

June She's pulling out all the stops ... (*She opens the door to the hall*)

Sarah enters, wearing an even sexier dress, more close fitting, more plunging, obviously new

There's an uncomfortable silence

June Sarah! That's a nice dress. Is it new?

Sarah A last throw of the dice, June.

June It's not needed. Tracey's gone.

Sarah I know. I met her in the drive. Apparently she's off to the Seychelles.

June (*after hesitating*) Where does that leave Paul?

Sarah (*coldly*) Not wanted on voyage.

June I meant where does it leave you and Paul?

Sarah No, you meant where does it leave Paul? I wasn't going anywhere.

June What are you going to do?

Frank I know what I'd do.

June I wasn't asking you, Frank.

Frank I'd kick his ecclesiastical arse straight out the door.

June Frank!

Sarah That was my first instinct, Frank. Then I remembered something ...

June What was that?

Sarah Tuscany.

Frank (*staring*) Tuscany?

Sarah June knows what I mean. He never had Tuscany — I did. It's made me a little more understanding.

Frank You're going to forgive him.

Sarah I said a *little* more, Frank.

June Did Tracey tell you about his new heart?

Sarah Yes. I must say that was a surprise. A woman's heart. I haven't detected anything feminine about him lately.

June I wondered if it would be strong enough.

Sarah A woman's heart! Strong enough? They're like teak — they have to be.

Sarah breaks off as Paul enters. He looks surprised at finding them there

Paul Oh. I didn't know. I'd better wait ... in the garden ... (*He half turns*)

Sarah If you're looking for Tracey — she's gone.

Paul (*turning*) Gone?

Sarah Off to the Seychelles with her sister. She's changed her mind.

Paul stares from one to the other

Paul What's come over me? I've gone mad. I've been such a fool.

Sarah You won't get any argument from me.

Paul What can I say?

Sarah (*silkily*) What about ... Gordon Bennett?

Paul I deserved that — and more. But it wasn't just me ... it was him.

Sarah Do you mean Melvin?

Paul Yes. He had this power. Some sort of possession. It was too strong.

Sarah It must have been — because he's not here.

Paul I know he's not here but his heart ——

Sarah That's not here either.

Paul (*staring*) Then, where is it?

Sarah Try Tunbridge Wells.

Paul I don't understand. If I haven't got his heart ... how do you explain what happened?

Sarah How do you explain it?

June (*quickly*) It must have been the medication — the strong drugs.

Paul Yes. That's what it was. I must have been drugged.

Sarah slowly holds up drug dispenser

Sarah You haven't been taking your medication. I checked. You haven't taken your pills since you came here. Did you think they'd slow you down?

Paul No. I was confused, disorientated. I thought I'd taken them ... But you weren't here to remind me ...

June Paul could be suffering from the effects of *not* taking them.

Paul That's it! The effect of being suddenly deprived.

Frank Whatever problems you've had this week, Paul — I don't think deprivation is one of them.

June gives Frank a sharp glance

Sarah So that's your explanation, is it? You didn't know what you were doing. You couldn't help yourself.

Paul looks into the accusing faces for a moment

Paul (*finally*) No. No, I could help myself. But you're wrong about Melvin. He was here. He haunted me. She never stopped talking about him. How he lived his life. The things he did. I knew more about his life than I did my own. And what a life. He did things I'd never dare to do — things I never dreamt of. Incredible, mad things. And he didn't give a damn. I couldn't stop thinking about him. He preyed on my mind. I've always done the right thing. He never did the right thing. I've always done my duty. I did my duty to my parents, to the church, to my family, to the sick and needy. I came from a long line of clergymen. I married a bishop's daughter. I led a blameless existence. If I died under the knife a few months ago I'd have died a good man. And then along came Melvin.

Sarah Don't you mean along came Tracey?

Paul I was weak.

Sarah (*shrugging*) Many are called but few are chosen, Paul. (*She takes Paul's clerical collar from her bag*) Put this on.

Paul finds himself holding his collar

You look ridiculous without it.

Paul Does this mean you forgive me?

Sarah No, it means we have two weddings and a funeral this week and we need the money.

Paul Can you ever forgive me?

Sarah (*after a pause*) We'll see. In the meantime we'll make a start with the beta-blockers ... (*She picks up the jug*)

Frank No!

Sarah What?

They all stare

Frank It's been a few days. I think he should be lying down to take them ...

Sarah You're right. How solicitous of you, Frank. We'll go to your room, Paul. (*She opens the door*)

Paul They make me sleepy.

Sarah Not a bad thing under the circumstances.

Sarah exits

Paul is about to follow

Frank Oh, Paul, about your new heart ...

Paul Yes.

Frank You've had a bit of a bonus. According to Tracey it belonged to a vicar.

Paul A vicar!

Frank Yes.

Paul If only I'd known. A vicar.

Frank The Reverend Frances Venables. Highly thought of, I believe, You'll probably find the entry in Crockfords.

Paul I'll look for it at once. You see, if I'd known, things might have been different.

Frank They would have been.

Paul It preyed on my mind.

Frank It's important to have the right mental attitude when you're ill. Isn't that right, June?

June (*bleakly*) Yes ...

Paul puts his hand on his heart

Paul Do you know, I begin to feel better already ... (*He turns back to the door*)

Frank Oh, Paul. When you look up the entry ... it's Frances with an e ...
Paul (*staring*) With an e? (*His expression of confusion turns to one of concern*)
Sarah (*off*) Sausage ...
Paul Coming ... Moppet ... (*With a second worried glance towards Frank*) With an e ...?
Frank With an e.

Paul looks uncertain for a moment. The penny drops

Paul Gordon Bennett!

He exits looking stunned

June Did you have to tell him that? Suppose his body rejects it?
Frank It hasn't up to now.
June He hasn't known up to now. And he's against women priests.
Frank That's the joke.

June crosses behind Frank, picks up the jug and looks for a glass

What was that about Tuscany?
June Tuscany?
Frank She said you'd know what she meant.
June So do you.
Frank I've never been to Tuscany.
June It's a metaphor.
Frank Oh. (*Pause*) What for?
June Sex.
Frank I knew it! You haven't forgiven me.
June I have.
Frank Then stop reminding me. (*Pause*) Do you think she'll forgive him?
June Why not? She's a bishop's daughter. And that's what the church is all about. Blessed is the sinner who repenteth ...
Frank Well, by the look in her eye he's going to repenteth.

June is about to pour from the jug. Frank turns to see her and starts from his chair

What are you doing? That's for patients. (*He struggles to her and snatches the jug from her*)
June It's only water.

Frank No, it isn't. It's gone off. It's been standing too long ... (*He staggers to the garden door*)

June watches, fascinated. Frank throws the contents of the jug into the garden

Oh. (*He waves apologetically*) Sorry. (*He turns*)
June Frank! You forgot your walking frame.
Frank What?
June You're on your feet.
Frank I'm holding on.
June But you're walking!
Frank I'm staggering.
June You're unsteady but you're upright.
Frank (*considering*) I am feeling stronger ...
June You couldn't have done that last week. It's a miracle.
Frank It's the steroids.
June You've been taking them for months. This is recent. This is since ——
Frank Since when?
June Since Paul ——
Frank Don't you dare.
June Prayed for you.
Frank He isn't the only one. What about the sewing circle?
June They've moved on.
Frank I didn't know that.
June I didn't like to tell you. They found you unresponsive.
Frank What about Aunt Marion in South Africa? I thought she had a direct line.
June She couldn't get through.
Frank Well, perhaps the girls ...
June (*staring*) After the way you've raised them? They're heathens. They worship the sun!
Frank Well, what about you ...?
June (*softly*) There's always been me, Cookie. I go back further than the steroids. No, this has happened since Paul added his voice.
Frank But he's a phony.
June Perhaps. But you heard what Sarah said. "Many are called but few are chosen." Perhaps Paul's been chosen.
Frank I doubt God would listen to him.
June All I know is that you could hardly move last week. I'm going to get your coat. We're going to have a walk around the garden. You can take my arm. We'll be seen out together ...

Frank I'll fall over.
June You won't. You'll see .. (*She picks up the jug*) After this, we'll get
  Paul to mention your prostate ...

  June exits

*Frank flexes his arms thoughtfully. He struggles to the desk. He regards
one of the heavy books. He takes a deep breath and raises it with one
hand. He replaces it. He places another book on top of the first. He adds
a third and then a fourth. Using both hands he raises them. He is now
holding a pile of books. He looks upwards in silent gratitude. He mouths
the word "thanks". The books suddenly spill on the floor*

Frank Bugger! (*He looks cautiously from side to side. He looks up once
  more to the heavens. He shrugs and gives a wry smile*) Sorry.

CURTAIN

FURNITURE AND PROPERTY LIST

ACT I
SCENE 1

On stage: Easy chairs
Stool
Cushions
Two coffee tables. *On them*: Thermos jug of water, glasses, heavy volume
Desk. *On it*: heavy books
Bookcase
Pair of crutches
Collapsed wheelchair
Bell
Heavy curtains either side of door leading out into gardens

Off stage: Walking frame (**Frank**)
Shopping bag (**June**)

ACT I
SCENE 2

On stage: As before

Off stage: Half-empty bottle of vodka, handbag (**Sarah**)

ACT II
SCENE 1

Set: Newspaper

Off stage: Small motorized buggy with horn, tablet dispenser (**June**)
Cigarette packet (**Sarah**)
Paul's clerical collar (**Tracey**)

ACT II
SCENE 2

Strike: Wheelchair

Off stage: Drug dispenser, handbag containing **Paul**'s clerical collar (**Sarah**)

LIGHTING PLOT

Property fittings required: nil

ACT I, SCENE 1

To open: General interior lighting

No cues

ACT I, SCENE 2

To open: General interior lighting

No cues

ACT II, SCENE 1

To open: General interior lighting

No cues

ACT II, SCENE 2

To open: General interior lighting

No cues

EFFECTS PLOT

ACT I

Cue 1   **Frank**: "I thought not."   (Page 4)
            Sound of church bells

ACT II

Cue 2   **Frank** sails backwards into the garden   (Page 40)
            Loud crash from outside

www.ingramcontent.com/pod-product-compliance
Lightning Source LLC
LaVergne TN
LVHW051803080426
835511LV00019B/3401